HELP!
I NEED A CHURCH

Jim Newheiser

Consulting Editor: Dr. Paul Tautges

Help! I Need a Church

© 2016 Jim Newheiser

ISBN
Paper: 978-1-63342-081-6
epub: 978-1-63342-082-3
Kindle: 978-1-63342-083-0

Published by **Shepherd Press**
P.O. Box 24
Wapwallopen, PA 18660

www.shepherdpress.com

All Scripture quotations, unless stated otherwise, are from the NASB Copyright © 1960, 1962, 1963, 1968, 1971, 1972, 1973, 1975, 1977, 1995 by The Lockman Foundation.

Designed by **documen**

Contents

INTRODUCTION

In over twenty years of working at a biblical counseling center, I have observed that the single greatest impediment to our counselees making progress is their lack of a proper relationship with a solid biblical church. Sometimes the fault is with the local church which fails to shepherd and, if necessary, discipline the sheep. Some local churches shirk their biblical responsibilities and look exclusively to outside counselors to care for their troubled members. Often, however, the problem lies with the counselees, who have never committed themselves to a solid biblical church. Consequently, when crises arise they don't have access to the resources and help God provides for his people in the local assembly of believers. Sometimes people turn to outside counselors as substitute pastors. One of the most important things a biblical counselor can do in such situations is to help counselees establish a committed relationship with a solid local church where they can enjoy the ongoing privileges of both being cared for and caring for others. While a crisis is not the ideal time to look for a church, God may use such a trial to draw his people to a biblical church where they will be blessed (and will be a blessing) for many years to come.

There are various reasons why professing Christians are not well connected to a biblical church. We have observed situations like the following:[1]

Richard and Jodie have attended a popular church for a few years, being drawn to the moving worship music, the dynamic (and funny) pastor, and the programs which their kids love. Several weeks ago, their fourteen-year-old daughter, Michelle, started sneaking out at night with her boyfriend, apparently engaging in substance abuse and immorality. Jodie tried to confront Michelle, who became very angry. The encounter turned into a shouting match. Richard tried to intervene, taking Michelle's side, saying that Jodie was too harsh. Now Jodie and Richard are hardly speaking to each other. They called the church asking for family counseling. The church office said that the pastors don't do counseling, but they refer members to Christian psychologists in the area.

Richard was hoping that the Bible had answers for their situation. Jodie was concerned about the cost of the counseling.

Dan and Darla have been married for thirty years. Active in their local church, Dan served for years as a deacon and Darla led the women's ministry. Three years ago, the church where they had been members for over twenty years experienced a terrible split. It seemed that the people on both sides were ugly and vindictive. Dan and Darla were heartbroken. It was like going through a divorce. They finally left their church. For months they didn't even bother going to church. Now they occasionally attend the mega-church in their community, arriving just as the service begins and slipping out during the last song. Both of them feel so disillusioned that they have determined never again to join a church. The risk of getting hurt again is just too great. They have even considered the possibility of having their own little worship service at home on Sundays.

James and Sally attend a growing new church which currently meets in a school. Sally sings on the worship team while James helps to lead a homegroup. Over time, however, James noticed that Sally seemed to be getting close to one of the men on the worship team and even saw them holding hands after a rehearsal. James confronted Sally, who confessed that she and Sam, the bass player, spend hours talking and enjoy a connection that she has never felt with James. She claims they haven't had sex, but she admits they have kissed on occasion. She doesn't want to give up her "soul mate." James, after trying unsuccessfully to confront Sam, approached Phil, the Senior Pastor. At first Phil was reluctant to do anything, saying, "You don't have proof that they have committed adultery. Furthermore, Sam is our only bass player. I really can't afford to lose him." When James protested, Phil finally agreed that Sally and Sam probably shouldn't remain on the worship team. James then asked Phil if the church leadership would do anything else about the situation. Phil replied, "We are a young church. We aren't ready to start practicing church discipline yet."

John and Cindy were growing in their faith, mainly through reading solid Christian books and listening to expository sermons on the Internet. They decided that they needed to leave their seeker-sensitive mega-church and find an assembly more in keeping with their new convictions. After carefully researching online the doctrinal statements of various churches, John and Cindy decided to join a small church which featured much deeper expository sermons. At first, John and Cindy were happy in their new church home, where people seemed much more serious about their faith. But over time a few things have started to bother them. Their new church seems to place very little emphasis on evangelism. The leaders rule with an iron hand, sometimes even trying to control church members' personal decisions about issues of Christian freedom. What most disturbs John and Cindy is that when a family leaves the church, the pastor criticizes them publicly, almost branding them as traitors. John and Cindy wonder if they have made a big mistake by joining this little church.

In this mini-book we'll be looking at what the Bible says about the local church, and we'll find answers to some of the problems faced by these couples.

1
Why You Need a Local Church

We have seen many of the difficulties associated with church life. Church members, including the leaders, are still sinners. Conflicts will take place. People will let you down. Feelings will get hurt. Some wonder, "Why do we need the church if we already have our own relationship with Christ?" Others criticize the institution of the local church and seek to establish alternative ministries to fill its place. If we go to the Bible, however, we find the following teachings that show why we need to be part of a local church.

The Church Is Important

Our Lord Jesus Christ established the church as the institution through which he would accomplish his work in the age between his ascension and his return.

I will build My church;² and the gates of
Hades will not overpower it.

(Matthew 16:18)

This is good news! In spite of the weaknesses and
failings of those in the church, Jesus himself is
the true church builder. Though local churches
and denominations may come and go, Jesus will
not allow his church to fail. When one church or
denomination turns away from the gospel, Jesus
raises up another.

Jesus cares deeply for his church, which he bought
with his own blood (Acts 20:28). The church is
portrayed as his cherished bride (Ephesians 5:25)
and his dwelling place (1 Corinthians 3:16–17). The
church universal, which consists of all believers in
every age, is expressed through many individual
local churches. The apostle Paul also explains the
importance of the local church by calling it

the household of God, which is the
church of the living God, the pillar and
support of the truth.

(1 Timothy 3:15)

The local church is God's chosen agent for
missions and evangelism, as illustrated by the

church in Antioch which sent Paul and Barnabas on the first missionary journey (Acts 13:1–3). This work of missions focuses upon not merely gaining converts, but also establishing local churches in every city (Acts 14:23).

You Need the Church

When God delivers us from the world and places us into his glorious kingdom by the gospel, in his wisdom he typically incorporates us into a community of believers. In the book of Acts we read how new converts were immediately added to a local church (Acts 2:47). The idea of a churchless Christian is unthinkable in the New Testament. Believers are referred to as sheep who are members of God's flock. As sheep we all need to be shepherded and fed. God has appointed pastors/elders/overseers[3] to care for his sheep in local churches/flocks. Paul tells the Ephesian elders,

> Be on guard for yourselves and for all
> the flock, among which the Holy Spirit
> has made you overseers, to shepherd the
> church of God which He purchased with
> His own blood.
>
> (Acts 20:28)

Some believers claim that they can be fed the Word simply by listening to sermons online or reading good books. The shepherding described in the New Testament, however, does not consist merely of preaching, but is also personal and relational. We all need loving, Christlike shepherds to keep us accountable, to help protect us from sin and error, to counsel and encourage us in times of trouble, to equip us to serve the Lord (Ephesians 4:11–12), and to minister the Word to us, both publicly and privately (Acts 20:20). While biblical counselors outside the church may use their expertise to assist a church in helping its members through a crisis, such counselors can never replace the ongoing shepherding and discipleship functions of the local church.[4] Though it is good to praise God individually and as families, God also calls upon us to enjoy the privilege of assembling with his people in the church to worship him (Hebrews 10:25; Acts 2:42; 20:7; Ephesians 5:19; Psalm 111:1). Our gathering together to worship our Savior is a taste of heaven (Revelation 5:11–14)! For a believer, to be away from worship among God's people is a source of sorrow (Psalm 42:4).

The Church Needs You

The Lord places you in the local church so you can serve him and his people. Just as every part of a human body is important, so every believer has a vital part to play in the local church body (1 Corinthians 12:7, 14–26). Through the church we enjoy the privilege of loving others by meeting practical needs (Acts 2:44–45), using our spiritual gifts to build one another up (Romans 12:4–8), and mutually encouraging one another (Romans 15:14; Ephesians 4:15; Hebrews 3:13; 10:24).

> *Be devoted to one another in brotherly love ... contributing to the needs of the saints, practicing hospitality ... Rejoice with those who rejoice, and weep with those who weep.*
>
> (Romans 12:10, 13, 15)

Those who don't give themselves to a local church end up robbing their brothers and sisters of the gift that God intends for them to be to his people.

Must You Join a Church?

Many refuse to join a local church because they don't like to make commitments or be under authority. Others argue that they don't want to join a church because church membership is not explicitly mentioned in the Bible. Some professing Christians, rather than committing to a particular local church, enjoy visiting different churches from week to week (or no church at all if they don't feel like getting out of bed on Sunday morning). Does the Bible speak to these situations?

Consider that while the word "Trinity" is not used in the New Testament, the concept of God's Tri-unity is clearly biblical; likewise, the term "church member" may not be explicitly used in the New Testament, but the concept behind church membership is clearly biblical. In 1 Corinthians 12:12 Paul uses the word "members," in the sense of the parts of a human body, to illustrate how each believer is an integral part of the church. Church membership means that a believer is committed to a particular local church where he or she will assemble with others for worship (Hebrews 10:25), where the believer will use his or her spiritual gifts to build up the local body (1 Peter 4:10–11), whose people the believer will love (1 John 4:7–8), and to whose leaders he or she will submit (1 Thessalonians 5:12–13). The author to the Hebrews writes,

> Obey your leaders and submit to them, for they keep watch over your souls as those who will give an account. Let them do this with joy and not with grief, for this would be unprofitable for you.
>
> (Hebrews 13:17)

Church leaders are told that they will give an account for the sheep that God has entrusted to them (1 Peter 5:2–3). Church membership is a means of identifying which sheep are in a particular flock for which its elders have responsibility. The practice of biblical church discipline also implies membership. Paul says that we cannot judge outsiders, but only those within the church. You can't be put out if you were never in (1 Corinthians 5:12–13). If you are a professing Christian who refuses to join a local church, who keeps watch over your soul? To whom are you accountable according to Hebrews 13:17?[5] By not joining a church you are, in effect, conveying that you don't need accountability.

To remain aloof from commitment to the local

church is therefore to disobey Scripture. It has sometimes been said that those who want all of the benefits of church membership without taking on the commitment are essentially "dating the church," like a man who wants the benefits of having a girlfriend without making the commitment of marriage. Others have likened these professing believers to spiritual hitchhikers who want a free ride without taking their share of responsibility.[6]

While it is clear, then, that the Bible teaches church membership, living this out may differ from church to church. Some churches have written membership covenants. It is even possible for a church with no formal membership process to identify and care for those who are committed to the body, thus creating a *de facto* membership.

Membership Has Its Privileges

The person who never commits to a local church will never fully enjoy the blessings of being an integral part of a church family. His or her opportunities for service in ministry will probably be limited. Why would a church allow a person who is uncommitted and unaccountable to teach a class or lead a ministry?

Believers in the early church were committed

to one another, including during times of personal or financial crisis (Acts 2:44–45; 4:32; 2 Corinthians 8–9). A godly local church will help its faithful members with benevolence in times of need. It is not reasonable, however, for a person to expect that a church to which he or she is not committed will be committed to him or her in the same way it is to its own members. Most churches can't offer significant help to people who are not committed and whom they don't know well, both because they don't have the resources and because of the warnings against helping those who refuse to be diligent (2 Thessalonians 3:6–13).[7] Similarly, when church members face a spiritual crisis, the leaders of their church should be committed to invest effort sacrificially to counsel them biblically and to walk through their trial with them. Sheep that are not committed to any flock may find it much harder to get the same level of care in a crisis.[8]

Commitment to a Local Church Requires Grace

It has often been said that there is no perfect church. But nor is there any perfect church member. As the old joke goes, if you find a perfect church you shouldn't join it, because if you do it won't be perfect anymore. Whenever sinners work together in close quarters, whether in churches or in families, conflict and disappointment will arise. However, God uses the challenges and trials which take place in these relationships to refine and sanctify us to be more like Christ (James 1:2–4). So rather than giving up and writing off our brothers and sisters, we have the privilege of reflecting God's grace as we learn to

> accept one another, just as Christ also
> accepted us to the glory of God.
> (Romans 15:7)

So, having seen that being part of a church is biblical, how should we go about choosing a church? We will think about this question in the rest of this mini-book.

2
How Not to Choose a Church

Many people are looking for love in all the wrong places. Likewise, one of the main reasons why Christians fail to enjoy the great blessings God desires to give his people through the church is that their choice of a church is not based upon biblical priorities. I often ask counselees in search of a local church to make a list, in order of priority, of what is most important to them. I ask others why they chose their particular church. Common responses include the following:

» I want a church at which I enjoy the music style (whether traditional or contemporary).

» I want a church with lots of programs which my children will enjoy (or I want a church which has no children's programs).

» I want to go to a church where I already have lots of friends (or I want to make a fresh start and meet new people).

» I want a preacher who is easy to listen to because he is … (funny, deep, not too deep, etc.).

» I want a church with an attractive facility (or which meets in a home).

» I want to go to a small (or large) church.

» I want to go to a church where there are people like us—in terms of age, social class, ethnicity, and so on. (Or I want to go to a church where there are people who are different!)

» I want to go to a church that is casual (or that is formal).

» I want to go to a church where people are politically involved (or not involved).

» I want to go to a church with lots of single people my age so I can find a spouse.

While each of these factors may play a secondary role in church choice, none holds biblical importance. Scripture does not prescribe a particular music style, size of a local church, or level of formality. The Bible teaches that the spiritual instruction of children is primarily the responsibility of parents (Deuteronomy 6:7-9;

Proverbs 1:8; 4:1). Any children's programs in the local church merely supplement the instruction given by parents. Children who may not yet be believers and may be most attracted to fun and food should not dictate where the family goes to worship God.

So if these aren't the criteria for choosing a church, what are?

3

What to Look for in a Church

Sometimes I challenge a believer whose list includes some of the criteria mentioned in the previous chapter to make a new list based solely upon Scripture (with Bible references for each item). I believe the most important factors include the following ten points.

1. Is This Church Centered on the Gospel of Jesus Christ?

When I visit a church, I often ask myself, "What is this church all about?" You can tell what really matters by what is emphasized from the pulpit, discussed by the people, and even displayed on the walls. Sometimes I will ask ordinary members, "Why do you go to this church?" Some churches are all about the music. Some like a church because it supports home-schooling or a Christian school, because of the great kids' programs, or even because it has no programs for children and youth. Some attend a church because of a famous preacher, or because the *right people*, including celebrities, go there. Some like a church because of the political activism of its members. Some churches focus on their heritage in church history or a confession of faith.

But Paul tells the Corinthians,

> *I determined to know nothing among you except Jesus Christ, and Him crucified.*
> (1 Corinthians 2:2)

The best answer I could hear from a church member as to what his or her church was about would be, "I attend this church because it is centered on the glorious gospel of Jesus Christ." This gospel-centeredness will pervade every aspect of church life. The preaching will focus upon the gospel and upon Christ's glory, not upon the leader's charisma (John 3:29–30). The worship will exalt God's grace in the gospel. The relationships will reflect God's love to us in the gospel. The basis of acceptance into the church will be fellowship in the gospel (Romans 15:7). And the evangelistic outreach and other programs and activities of the church will seek to further the work of the gospel. The aroma of the gospel permeates a healthy church.

2. Does This Church Stand Firm on Sound Biblical Doctrine?

You can get an idea of what a church believes by reading its doctrinal statement or confession of faith, but you also need to listen carefully to what is actually preached and taught to see if it is standing firm on biblical doctrine (Titus 1:9; 2:1). Some churches have strayed from their biblical heritage. The most important doctrine on which a church must be clear is that of salvation (Galatians 1:8):

»   Who is God? Does this church have a high and biblical view of God's attributes and his supreme glory (Acts 17:24–29; Romans 11:33–36)?

»   Who is man? Does this church believe that we are basically good or bad? Scripture teaches that we are sinners who deserve God's wrath (Romans 3:23; 6:23).

»   Who is Jesus? Scripture teaches that Jesus is fully God and fully man (John 1:1–2, 14; Colossians 2:9). Jesus lived a perfect life, died on the cross as our substitute, paying the penalty for all who believe in him (2 Corinthians 5:21; 1 Peter 3:18), and has been raised from the dead (1 Corinthians 15:3–4).

» Are we saved by our works or by God's grace? The Bible declares that our salvation is God's work: we are saved by his grace alone, through faith alone, in Christ alone (Ephesians 2:8–9; Romans 3:21–26; Galatians 2:16). The person who believes in Christ immediately gains perfect status with God, having the righteousness of Christ imputed to him or her. There is nothing the believer can do to add to or take away from this status (Philippians 3:9). Our works and religious ceremonies (including baptism and communion) do not contribute anything to our soul's salvation.

As well as this, a church should also affirm that the Bible is inspired (God-breathed—2 Timothy 3:16) and inerrant—the sole authority for faith and practice. A church must also affirm the sufficiency of Scripture to equip us for every good work for life and godliness (2 Timothy 3:17; 2 Peter 1:3), as opposed to relying upon worldly philosophies and psychologies to address spiritual issues (Colossians 2:8–9; Romans 12:1–2).

What about the rest of the church's doctrine?

In addition to these central doctrines you will want to know what a church teaches in areas such as election versus free will, baptism (believers' baptism or infant baptism), prophecy (premillennial, amillennial, etc.), and spiritual gifts such as tongues and prophecy (cessationist or continuationist).

Do you have to agree about everything? As long as there is a fundamental agreement on the main issues of salvation and biblical authority you may be able to get along in a church with which you differ on other doctrines. It actually would be unusual for independent thinkers to agree with a given church on every single point of doctrine. It may also be that there are some points of doctrine on which you are not yet settled. How flexible you can be will depend upon what you can tolerate in terms of teaching or practice. Also, consider how flexible the church is in terms of allowing members or leaders (if you aspire to leadership) to hold different views on less central doctrines. If your doctrinal differences would keep you from being able to join the church or use your gifts to serve, you probably should look elsewhere.

3. Is the Bible Faithfully Preached Week after Week?

Paul exhorts Timothy,

> *I solemnly charge you in the presence of God and of Christ Jesus, who is to judge the living and the dead, and by His appearing and His kingdom: preach the word; be ready in season and out of season; reprove, rebuke, exhort, with great patience and instruction. For the time will come when they will not endure sound doctrine; but wanting to have their ears tickled, they will accumulate for themselves teachers in accordance to their own desires.*
>
> (2 Timothy 4:1-3)

What Paul warned against has happened in our day. Many popular preachers tell people what they want to hear and leave out the parts of Scripture that might be upsetting or challenging. Some preachers are mere storytellers, pop-psychologists, or philosophers. The most important thing about a preacher, however, is not his humor or even eloquence, but his faithfulness (2 Timothy 2:2).

A faithful preacher preaches only the Word of God, his sole authority. He also preaches all of the Word—the whole counsel of God (Acts 20:27), including the difficult parts about God's holy wrath against sin. A faithful preacher doesn't merely encourage, but he also reproves and rebukes sin.

All faithful preaching will be grounded in the gospel (what God has done for us). Paul said that he was eager to go to Rome to preach the gospel to believers (Romans 1:15). As believers we need to hear the gospel weekly in order to be grounded in our new identity in Christ, which will motivate and enable us to live in light of what God has done for us (Romans 6:11; 2 Corinthians 5:17). Each of us, including preachers, has ideas about what should be emphasized in preaching—gospel versus law, encouragement verses correction, and so on. Because Scripture itself is perfectly balanced, I believe that the best approach is to preach through books of the Bible or extended sections of Scripture. Over time this will reflect what the Bible emphasizes. When you visit a church, ask yourself these questions: Is this preaching faithful to the Word of God? Is the gospel undergirding every sermon? Are those who preach gifted by God (1 Timothy 3:2)? Is this a place where my family could be fed the Word of God week after week?

4. Is the Worship Biblical and God-Centered?

The most important Person we are to seek to please in our worship is God himself. He seeks worshipers who worship in spirit (sincerely and from the heart) and in truth (John 4:23–24). Not all worship is acceptable to God (Isaiah 1:14; Matthew 15:8–9). Under the Old Covenant, God precisely prescribed the way his people were to worship him. Those who violated the holiness of his worship sometimes paid a deadly price (Leviticus 10:1–3). God's worship is still holy under the New Covenant. Some in the early church who did not respect God's holiness in worship became sick and others died (1 Corinthians 11:29–31; Acts 5:1–10).

The New Testament also reveals how we are to worship God under the New Covenant. The teaching of the apostles and the practice of the early church provide the model.

> *They were continually devoting*
> *themselves to the apostles' teaching and*
> *to fellowship, to the breaking of bread*
> *and to prayer.*
>
> *(Acts 2:42)*

Worship should include the reading and proclamation of Scripture (1 Timothy 4:13; 2 Timothy 4:1–4)[9] and prayer (1 Timothy 2:8). The early church also praised God in song (Ephesians 5:19; Colossians 3:16) and faithfully practiced the ordinances of the Lord's Supper (many believe they did this weekly, Acts 2:42; 20:7; 1 Corinthians 11:23–26) and water baptism. Missions reports and testimonies also took place when the church gathered (Acts 14:27).

Because worship is regulated by Scripture a church should have a biblical basis for any element which is included in worship. It is also important to distinguish between the essential elements (or components) of worship and the circumstances of worship (i.e., meeting time or music style) in which we have freedom (and preferences). Sadly, many churches don't even think seriously about studying the Bible to know what should be included in worship. As a result, they end up following their own traditions in worship, which often include added unbiblical ceremonies and sacraments (Matthew 15:3, 9). Others plan their worship primarily for the purpose of attracting unsaved visitors.[10] This man-centered focus can be harmful in worship as many churches will de-emphasize or leave out elements which the Bible says are important. Unbelievers are usually not attracted by long prayer times and meaty Bible exposition, so sermons become short and funny, and prayers are very brief. The result is that the people of God don't receive the spiritual feeding they need and corporate prayer is neglected.

Music is often viewed as a way to draw outsiders. Music is a very powerful means by which God can be worshiped and his people can have their hearts stirred while also learning truth. But some worship services degenerate into concerts. The songs that are chosen often fall short of the biblical examples of God-centered praise (Psalm 66:5–7; 95:6; 96:8–9; 100:1–5). Often extra elements, such as movies, dance, and drama, are added to seeker-focused worship services.

While such activities may be appropriate at other times,[11] they are not prescribed in Scripture and, therefore, detract from precious time which should be given to the biblical elements of worship.

Having said this, I am not saying that a church should ignore lost visitors or be *seeker-insensitive*. Worship should be intelligible and orderly (1 Corinthians 14:33). It is appropriate to address the lost with the gospel in the sermon. But we are not to entertain them. William Still wrote,

> The pastor is called to feed the sheep, even if they do not want to be fed. He is certainly not to become an entertainer of goats. Let goats entertain goats, and let them do it out in goatland. You will certainly not turn goats into sheep by pandering to their goatishness.[12]

Paul describes a situation in which evangelism may be a byproduct of worship:

> If all prophesy, and an unbeliever or an ungifted man enters, he is convicted by all, he is called to account by all; the secrets of his heart are disclosed; and so he will fall on his face and worship God, declaring that God is certainly among you.
>
> (1 Corinthians 14:24–25)

In this scenario, the person who is converted in a worship service doesn't say, "I feel so comfortable and entertained here! It is just like TV!" Instead, he or she says, in effect, "What you are doing here is different from anything I have ever experienced. Surely God is among you! I too must fall down in reverence before this glorious God whom you worship!"

In summary, God-centered worship is a blessed and joyful privilege (1 Peter 2:5, 9). The key question about worship should not be "How did I like this service?" or "How did it make me feel?" but "Was God worshiped in spirit and in truth?"

5. Are the Leaders Biblically Qualified and Mutually Accountable?

Church leadership in our day often seeks to reflect the charisma, drive, and vision which our culture looks for in leaders in business or politics. "Successful" Christian leaders (meaning those with large churches and ministries) write books on leadership which seem based more upon management and marketing techniques than upon Scripture. In these models, the leader is regarded as the key to success. The New Testament, however, makes it clear that the Head and Chief Shepherd (Senior Pastor) of the church is Christ (1 Peter 5:4; Ephesians 1:22; 5:23) and that leaders are under-shepherds. The men who lead the church are simply workers in God's vineyard

serving under Jesus who makes his church grow
(1 Corinthians 3:5–9). Church leaders who are
concerned about building their own kingdom
detract from the glory of Christ, who taught us
to be servants (John 13:1–17; Mark 10:43). Their
attitude should be like that of John the Baptist:

> He [Christ] must increase, but I
> must decrease.
>
> (John 3:30)

Biblical leadership has more to do with character
than charisma. Leaders must be godly, humble,
mature believers who are above reproach, whose
families are in order and who set an example to the
flock (1 Timothy 3:1–7). Many of the qualifications
have to do with their ability to work with others:

> ... not ... pugnacious, but gentle,
>   peaceable ...
> ... not self-willed, not quick tempered ...
>   but ... self-controlled.
>
> (1 Timothy 3:3; Titus 1:7–8)

An unqualified leader will always want to get
his own way and will not defer to others. Such
men will go to great lengths to maintain their

power, even driving out those who question their authority or going across town to start their own church (3 John 9–10).

The biblical pattern is for a church to have a plurality of mutually accountable elders/pastors/overseers (Acts 14:23; 20:17; Titus 1:5). This provides a means by which a wayward pastor/elder can be held accountable and, if need be, disciplined by his fellow elders (1 Timothy 5:19–22; Acts 20:28–30). Also, the plurality of elders keeps the focus on Christ as the Head of his church. Finally, because Scripture teaches that the church is to be led by men (1 Timothy 2:12–14; 3:1–2), you should be wary of a church that has women serving as elders and pastors. Those who ignore these scriptural teachings are following culture rather than God's Word.

So when you visit a church you will want to find out about the church leadership. Are the leaders humble men whose gifts and character meet the biblical standards expressed in 1 Timothy 3:1–7 and Titus 1:5–9?

6. Do the Leaders/Pastors Shepherd the Sheep?

Both Paul and Peter exhort church leaders to shepherd God's flock (Acts 20:28; 1 Peter 5:2). Church leaders are reminded that they will give an account to God for how they have tended the sheep he entrusted to their care (Hebrews 13:17). Ezekiel 34 tells of the wicked shepherds in Israel who did not care for the sheep, but instead selfishly used and abused them. It is not enough for a church to have sound doctrine and for the preaching to be faithful to Scripture; the leaders must also be committed to emulating Jesus, the Good Shepherd who gave his life for his sheep (John 10:11). Some leaders are so driven to grow the church by attracting more people and resources that they don't have time to actually get involved in helping the hurting sheep that are already part of the flock. Many pastors refuse to invest time in counseling individuals and families through conflicts and crises. Some don't even believe that they are called to do so, but refer their members to outside "professional counselors" who may offer unbiblical advice.

Does the church you are visiting believe in the sufficiency of Scripture to give gospel-centered solutions for the spiritual problems believers face

(2 Timothy 3:16–17), or does it send its struggling people to outside psychologists? Are the leaders committed and equipped to minister God's Word, not just publicly before a crowd, but also to individuals and families who need comfort and encouragement (Acts 20:20)? This does not mean that the preaching pastor is the only one who will help troubled people. The benefit of having a plurality of elders/pastors is that many men are called and gifted to care for God's sheep. The work of caring for God's sheep should also be shared by many members in the church (Romans 15:14), including women equipped to care for other women (Titus 2:3–5).

7. Does This Church Practice Biblical Church Discipline?

Jesus is deeply concerned about the purity of his church, both in doctrine and in practice. He is also concerned about the influence that doctrinal error and immorality may have on others in the church.

> A little leaven leavens the whole lump of dough.
>
> (1 Corinthians 5:6)

Jesus teaches a process by which church discipline should take place (Matthew 18:15–17) and tells us that such discipline takes place with his authority (Matthew 18:18–20). Following Christ's instruction, Paul rebukes the Corinthians for failing to maintain the purity of their church, and instructs them to

> remove the wicked man from
> among yourselves.
>
> (1 Corinthians 5:13)

In our day, local churches tend to go to one of two extremes when it comes to discipline. Most commonly fail to practice church discipline. Little or no effort is made to correct and, if necessary, remove members who are involved in immorality or other serious sin, or who promote false and divisive teaching. Some pastors will say, "We are trying to get people to come into our church, not drive them out"; or, "We know that someday we should implement church discipline, but we aren't ready yet"; or, "We don't want to get sued." Also, since many churches don't practice church membership it is hard to "put out" someone who isn't officially "in." Some churches, especially very large ones, don't really know those who regularly attend so they have no ability to keep track of them or to maintain accountability.[13]

Failure to practice biblical church discipline harms churches. False teachers draw others after them and divide the church. When nothing is done about members who engage in sexual immorality, others are more likely to imitate their bad example.

At the opposite extreme, a few churches, perhaps reacting against the laxness of the majority, are harsh in their discipline. They put people out for minor doctrinal differences or infractions. Ungodly leaders use discipline to protect themselves against those who threaten their power (3 John 9–10). Biblical church discipline is to be carried out in a gentle, loving, and orderly fashion with the purpose of restoring the wayward brother or sister (Galatians 6:1; 2 Corinthians 2:6–8; Matthew 18:12–15) and upholding the honor of Christ.

8. Does This Church Equip Its Members to Serve God?

Paul tells us that Christ has given the church

> pastors and teachers, for the equipping of
> the saints for the work of service, to the

building up of the body of Christ.
(Ephesians 4:11–12)

The church officers are not called to do all of the ministries, but rather they are called to equip each member to use his or her gifts to build up the church (1 Peter 4:10–11). Do the elders/ pastors at the church you are visiting encourage every member to serve? Are members free to use their gifts and even to start new ministries? Are the elders/pastors encouraging and training future leaders (2 Timothy 2:2)? Is this a church in which others will disciple you and you will have opportunity to disciple others? Is this a church where you will be able to flourish serving Christ and his people? Is this a church in which men and women are being encouraged and equipped to be godly husbands, wives, parents, employees, employers, and citizens (Ephesians 5:22–6:9; Romans 13:1–7)?

9. Does This Church Community Have a Culture of Grace, Love, and Peace?

Paul writes,

If possible, so far as it depends on you, be

> at peace with all men.
> Accept one another, just as Christ also
> accepted us to the glory of God.
> (Romans 12:8; 15:7)

God accepts us, not based upon outward appearance or even our works, but by his grace towards us in Christ. Are people accepted and welcomed into this church regardless of age, ethnicity, social background, spiritual weakness, or differences on secondary issues (such as educational choices for children, views on food and drink, the place of children and youth programs in the church, views of the end times/rapture, etc.)?

Because we are still sinners, you will never find a church in which there is no conflict. But is this church one in which members deal with their differences by showing grace toward one another (Proverbs 19:11; 1 Peter 4:8) and by pursuing peace (Romans 12:18; Hebrews 12:14)? Do people seek to resolve their conflicts in a direct, biblical, and gentle way (Matthew 18:15; Galatians 6:1), rather than participating in slander, gossip, and bullying? Do these people love one another and enjoy being together (John 15:12; Acts 2:46; Romans 12:10)? Do they practice hospitality (1 Peter 4:9)? Do they build one another up with their words (Ephesians 4:15, 29; Hebrews 3:13; 10:24)? Are the socially awkward and weak included and cared for (Hebrews 12:13; 1 Thessalonians 5:14)? Do the members of this church lovingly meet one another's material needs, especially those of widows (Acts 2:46; James 1:27)?

The structure by which fellowship outside of the worship services takes place will vary from church to church. Some smaller churches may have a mid-week meeting as a church family at which close fellowship can take place. Many churches have homegroups which meet during the week and whose members focus on meeting one another's needs. The point is not the programs, but that the biblical "one-another" commands are being practiced.

10. Does This Church Have an Outward Focus—Missions, Evangelism, and Church Planting?

Some churches are such close families that it is hard for an outsider to break into them. Other churches are so concerned about precision in their doctrine and practice that they expend more energy keeping the wrong people out than in welcoming those from the outside. Jesus has given us the great commission to bring his gospel to the world so that disciples can be made to serve and worship him (Matthew 28:18–20; Acts 1:8). Sadly, many churches grow primarily by attracting sheep from other local flocks. Is this church seeking to grow through conversions? Are members of this church encouraged and equipped to practice personal evangelism? Paul says,

> Let your speech always be with grace, as though seasoned with salt, so that you will know how you should respond to each person.
>
> (Colossians 4:6)

Most evangelism in the New Testament takes place not when unbelievers walk into the church meeting, but when believers go out into the world with the gospel. Do members of this church reflect God's compassion (Isaiah 45:22) by seeking to reach their neighbors with the gospel? Do they proclaim the biblical gospel without embarrassment or alteration, trusting God to bring forth fruit (Romans 1:16–17; 10:13–15)? Does this church have a reputation for doing good in the community (Galatians 6:10; Jeremiah 29:5–7)? Do the leaders of this church have a desire to plant more churches? What is their involvement in missions? The early church was committed to evangelizing faraway places. The church in Antioch sent Paul and Barnabas on their first missionary journey (Acts 13:1–3). Is this church committed to raising up and sending out missionaries? Is it willing to make sacrifices, just as the church in Antioch did, sending its best to promote the gospel in other nations? Does the church regularly pray for and care for the missionaries it supports? Are these missionaries doing gospel work? What percentage of the church budget goes towards missions and outreach?

4

Hard Questions about Choosing a Church

W e've now seen what you should be looking for in a church, but you may still have some questions, such as the following:

1. How Can You Find Out What a Church Is Really Like?

Many people start their church search online. Does the feel of the website convey that this church is all about the gospel? What does the doctrinal statement say about what the church believes? The lack of a doctrinal statement is a yellow warning flag. Download some of the sermons (one is not enough, because good preachers have bad days and vice versa). Is Scripture being faithfully expounded? Is Christ being exalted? Does this feed your soul? What does the website say about the church's worship, evangelism, training, counseling, shepherding, discipline, and so on?

If the church seems to check out, visit it for a few

weeks. Is the worship reverent, joyful, and God-centered? Are the people warm and welcoming? Is there an atmosphere of gospel grace? If you really want to get to know a church, attend meetings other than the main worship service. Go to a Sunday-school class. Attend the evening or mid-week service. Go to a homegroup or a men's or ladies' function. Talk to the members. Invite some of the church leaders and their wives into your home for a meal so that you can get to know them. Hear their testimonies and their vision for the church. Share your own testimony with them. Perhaps you could show them this mini-book and ask what they think!

2. What About Extra-Biblical Preferences?

As mentioned before, many people choose a church primarily based upon factors which are not important biblically, such as music style, children's programs, location, size, and where their friends attend. While the ten explicitly biblical factors should be your primary consideration in selecting a church, you are free to consider your preferences when choosing between equally excellent churches. It is similar to when choosing a spouse: a single believer should make biblical considerations primary, but he or she has freedom to take other preferences into consideration when choosing among godly people of the opposite sex.

One factor which is perhaps the most difficult to weigh is travel distance. It is desirable to attend a church close to home so that you can be involved in the lives of your brothers and sisters and so that you can invite unsaved friends and neighbors who wouldn't be willing to make a long drive. This situation becomes complicated, however, if you can't find a suitable church in your immediate community and would have to drive a considerable distance to attend a church which meets your biblically based criteria. The decision of how far to travel will depend upon several factors, including the following:

» How far short of the biblical ideal does the nearby church fall?

» Are you being too judgmental?

» Can you afford the time and money it would take to drive to the better church?

» Do you have small children for whom the drive might become very difficult (Colossians 3:21)?

» Are you willing to make the commitment

to make that drive more than once a week in order to participate in the life of the church body?

» Might you have opportunity to be an influence for good in the weaker nearby church?

» Are the opportunities for ministry in the more distant church worth the drive?

There is no easy formula for making a final decision. Ultimately, you must prayerfully follow your own conscience.

3. How Can You Make up Your Mind about When to Join a Church?

I have known couples who decided very quickly that they wanted to marry each other, while others needed years before taking the plunge. In the same way, I have seen people (often those who have been hurt in the past) attend a church for years before joining. I have seen others who did their research before they came to a given church and were ready to join within a week or two. I have also seen some of those who quickly committed to a church leave after just a few months because they decided that it wasn't what they were looking for after all.

Joining a church is a serious matter. You are placing yourself under the care and the feeding of its leaders and you are committing yourself to love and serve Christ alongside the brothers and sisters there. On the other hand, joining a church is not like a marriage, which it is sinful ever to leave (see below).[14] Because Scripture instructs each of us to be committed to a local church and because there are risks involved with being unattached to a local body, I believe that it is important for people who are not yet church members to make up their minds on a timely basis. No church will perfectly meet all of your criteria. You will need to extend grace to a church's members, just as they will need to show grace to you. Nor should you expect God to give you some kind of supernatural sign as to which church to join. He expects you to apply the biblical criteria and make the best decision you can.

4. What if a Family Can't Agree upon Which Church to Join?

Ideally, if the husband or father is a believer, he should demonstrate leadership in choosing the church in which the family worships. If it is a matter of preference, his wife should be willing to follow his lead, as long as the church he has chosen is biblical and evangelical in the essentials, even if the wife believes another church is better. If the husband wants to join a church which denies the gospel, the wife has a right respectfully to refuse to attend and to choose a biblical church.

We must obey God rather than men.
(Acts 5:29)

In the same way, even if her husband refuses to commit to a church, she has the right to join a local body of believers (Hebrews 10:25; 13:17). In such situations she should address her husband with gentleness and grace. As children approach adulthood, they may be attracted to a different church from that of their parents. While Mom and Dad may prefer that their young adult children who still live in the home join them in worship, they may choose to give them freedom to join a different church. In such a situation they should be thankful that their offspring want to attend an evangelical church.

5. When Is It Right to Change Churches?

We all know people who switch churches every couple of years or whenever they hear about a new assembly where the grass may be a bit greener. Actually, when they joined their previous church they were looking for blue grass, but now they must have green! When someone leaves a church body in which they have been blessed and in which they have loved and served, it is painful, both for them and for those they leave behind. If you do this, you leave a hole in your former church. It will take time to establish relationships and ministry in your new church. Such a decision should not be made lightly.

For example, if your church is basically solid and biblical (say, 85 on a scale of 100 of your scriptural understanding of what a church should be), and you hear about another church in the area which sounds better (perhaps 91 on the same scale), considerations of relationship and loyalty would indicate that it would probably be wise to stay. On the other hand, churches and people change. Churches sometimes stray from their biblical roots. Some members may decide to leave because their old church has drifted too far from the biblical standard of what a church should be (perhaps from an 80 to a 40).

It may also be that you have changed as your understanding about the church has been transformed by Scripture. You realize that your current church falls short of the scriptural standard to such an extent that you can no longer stay in good conscience. Before leaving, go to the church leadership to respectfully show them from Scripture how you believe the church should change, and offer to help. It may be that at that point they will be glad to see you go. When leaving a church, be direct, gentle, and honest. Don't just disappear; tell the leadership that you are leaving and why you are leaving. Where you can do so, express appreciation for the blessings you have received from them. Some church leaders become angry or upset when their members leave (though they don't seem to mind when people leave other churches to join them). While those who leave should be sympathetic to their former leaders, those who lead must recognize that the sheep belong not to them, but to Christ (Acts 20:28).

Conclusion

Let's see how the believers that we met at the beginning of this mini-book fared in finding a biblical church.

Richard and Jodie became convinced that they needed to leave their old church because of significant shortcomings in its doctrine and practice. They could no longer imagine inviting a visitor to hear such inconsistent preaching. After visiting various churches they settled on Faith Bible Church, at which they believed they would be faithfully led and fed. It was hard to leave their old friends, but it has been a blessing to hear the Word of God carefully expounded each week. Even though their previous church hadn't practiced church membership they were persuaded that they should become members. Regarding the rebellion of their fourteen-year-old daughter, Michelle, the elders of the church counseled them and found a godly woman in the church to meet regularly with Michelle. Richard and Jodie are also making friends with people of various ages and finding places to serve in their new church home.

Dan and Darla finally realized that in spite of the hurt and heartache they had experienced in their previous church, it was God's will that they find a new local body in which they could commit and serve. After visiting several churches and asking lots of questions, they settled on Grace Baptist Church. After attending and observing carefully for over a year, they finally asked to meet with the elders about membership. Dan and Darla expressed appreciation to the leaders for showing patience as they made up their minds. While they realize that no church is perfect or conflict-free, they have seen that the leaders exercise their authority gently and that the people love one another and know how humbly to seek peace when differences arise. Dan and Darla are excited about being a part of this special church family.

When **James'** church refused to discipline his wife, Sally, even after she moved in with Sam, James decided to leave and find a different church. He initially went to Christ Reformed Church because of their biblical counseling ministry. There a godly older man helped him to face this great trial in a biblical and gracious way. When

James decided to join the church, the elders contacted the leaders of his previous church to check that he had left in good standing. They also offered to help the leaders of James' old church work through the situation between James and Sally biblically, but the leaders of that church weren't interested. The elders then sought to contact Sally, offering the hope and reconciliation of the gospel. She came once for counsel, but in the end chose to stay with Sam. While James has found that many things about Christ Reformed Church differ from churches he has attended in the past, he is learning and is very thankful to be in a body which will stand with him in his trials.

As **John and Cindy** studied what the Bible says about the church, they came to realize that, while the doctrine of their new church was sound, the church leadership were overstepping their authority and were probably unqualified (1 Peter 5:3). Furthermore, this church had an atmosphere of legalism and fear, rather than grace. John and Cindy could never imagine inviting their friends or family members to such a church. The leaders were very upset when John and Cindy told them of their departure, even threatening church discipline and claiming they weren't leaving on biblical grounds. John and Cindy then approached the choice of their next church more carefully. After several months they settled on New Life Community Church. They were blessed by the gospel focus which came through in every aspect of church life, from the preaching to the relationships among the people in the church. The elders of New Life made contact with John and Cindy's previous church and determined that there were no valid grounds for church discipline. Now that they have been received as members, John and Cindy hope to be at New Life for many more years to come!

Personal Application Projects

1. How would you answer someone who says, "I want Jesus but I don't need the church"?

2. How would you answer someone who says, "I don't need to join the church because church membership is not in the Bible"?

3. List the five most important factors you would consider in choosing a church, and rank them in order of priority.

4. What would you want to know if a friend asked you if he or she should change churches?

5. What gifts has God given you through which you can serve him in the church?

6. Read through the book of Acts and answer the following questions:

    » What is the content of the gospel message?

    » What do you learn about how the church is to be run?

    » What do you learn about how the work of missions is to be carried out?

7. List ten things about your present church for which you can give thanks to God.

Where Can I Get More Help?

Books

Anyabwile, Thabiti M., *What Is a Healthy Church Member?* (Wheaton, IL: Crossway, 2007)

Crotts, John, *Loving the Church: God's People Flourishing in God's Family* (Wapwallopen, PA: Shepherd Press, 2010)

Dever, Mark, *Nine Marks of a Healthy Church* (Wheaton, IL: Crossway, 2000)

——, *What Is a Healthy Church?* (Wheaton, IL: Crossway, 2007)

Leeman, Jonathan, *Church Membership: How the World Knows Who Represents Jesus* (Wheaton, IL: Crossway, 2012)

Mack, Wayne A. and Dave Swavely, *Life in the Father's House: A Member's Guide to the Local Church* (Phillipsburg, NJ: P&R, 2006)

Web Resources

Association of Certified Biblical Counselors, www.biblicalcounseling.com

The Institute for Biblical Counseling and Discipleship, www.ibcd.org

9 Marks Ministries, www.9marks.org

ENDNOTES

1   The names and some of the details in these scenarios have been changed.

2   The word "church" is sometimes used of the church universal (as in Matthew 16:18) and sometimes of local churches. The church universal consists of all believers who are scattered in various local churches.

3   "Elder," "pastor," and "overseer" refer to the same office (Acts 20:17, 28; Titus 1:5, 7; 1 Peter 5:1–5).

4   The primary purpose of the biblical counseling center with which I am involved, IBCD (The Institute for Biblical Counseling and Discipleship), is not primarily to do lots of counseling, but to train people, especially church leaders, to use the Scriptures to help one another with their spiritual problems.

5   The authority of the elders is subordinate to Scripture and members' ultimate responsibility is to obey God (Acts 5:29).

6   Dave Harvey, *Rescuing Ambition* (Wheaton, IL: Crossway, 2010), 160.

7   Local churches are often visited by professing Christians who are seeking a handout. In my church we typically ask such people where they are members so that we can help them work with their local church leaders. Such people usually prove to be committed and accountable to no one (Hebrews 13:17; 2 Thessalonians 3:6–13).

8   For example, our church-based biblical counseling center is so overwhelmed with people seeking help (most of whom are not members of a church which

offers such biblical help) that we don't have the resources to get to each of them right away. Many have to be put on a waiting list. On the other hand, our pastors and counselors are available to members of their local churches at any time, day or night.

9 Some mistakenly think that the singing alone is worship and preaching comes after that. But hearing God's Word proclaimed is also worship.

10 Well-known books on church growth talk about planning a service for the target audience of unbelievers.

11 There is nothing inherently wrong with drama, movies, or dance in their proper place, just as there is nothing wrong with sports in their proper place. But just as it would not be appropriate to hold a tennis match during a worship service, so it is not appropriate to fill the precious time allotted to worship with elements not taught in Scripture. Christians are free to use their church building for a movie night on a Friday evening or put on a play or a talent show on a Saturday afternoon as long as these do not take the place of worship. Also, while all church members should be expected to attend worship (Hebrews 10:25), these other activities should be optional.

12 William Still, *The Work of the Pastor* (Fearn: Christian Focus, 2010), 23.

13 It is possible for large churches to do an effective job of shepherding and disciplining the church by assigning members to leaders/elders who are to keep track of them.

14 This is so unless for explicitly biblical grounds of adultery or abandonment by an unbelieving spouse.

BOOKS IN THE HELP! SERIES INCLUDE...

More titles in preparation

For current listing go to: www.shepherdpress.com/lifeline

About Shepherd Press Publications

» They are gospel driven.

» They are heart focused.

» They are life changing.

Our Invitation to You

We passionately believe that what we are publishing can be of benefit to you, your family, your friends, and your work colleagues. So we are inviting you to join our online mailing list so that we may reach out to you with news about our latest and forthcoming publications, and with special offers.

Visit:

www.shepherdpress.com/newsletter
and provide your name and email address.